HOUSES OF HOPE

A POETIC EXPLORATION OF TIME HOPE & HUMAN EXISTENCE

AMY CECILIA GRAINGER

HOUSES OF HOPE

AMY CECILIA GRAINGER

©2025 Amy Cecilia Grainger
All rights reserved.

First published 2025

No part of this publication may be reproduced, stored in a retrieval system, or transmitted in any form or by any means—electronic, mechanical, photocopying, recording, or otherwise—without prior written permission of the author.

Disclaimer:
This work reflects the author's philosophical inquiry and lived experience. It is intended for personal reflection and creative exploration only and does not constitute professional advice or instruction. Readers remain solely responsible for their own interpretations and actions.

Author:
Amy Cecilia Grainger

Published by
Souls of Ones Feet

Graphic Design & Cover:
Ged L. M. Buick
ISBN: 978-1-0683830-2-1

:

'There are houses, extravagant elusive houses,
that flow through the pace in your chest,
ancestral compassion at its best.'

"When transformation aligns with timelessness
There resides a space to breathe
Love and hope bring harmony
Patience aids to heal"

THE EVER EXPANDING NOW

BEGINNING
In the beginning there was dust, molecules and magic – a dance so extravagantly tragic, a collision, a composure, of a new world that grows older – the beginning – kept expanding – and now – times is not withstanding.

BRIDGE
Welcome to this poetic exploration of time, space, human existence and hope. Feel this book as a gift, a journey of from my heart to yours.

Release any expectations.

Allow yourself to travel – to unravel – to evolve as you explore!

BEACON
Allow the words of these explorations to illuminate the avenues of your time.

Feel love, feel peace, feel hope in your heart.

Be time.

BACK TO A BEGINNING
When we evolve time disintegrates - we uncover a space often reserved or overlooked - time does not end.

It infinitely- begins again.

CONTENT

THE EVER-EXPANDING NOW..7
MESSAGE FROM THE AUTHOR 11
INSPIRATION SURROUNDS US 14
THE UNSEEN CHAMBERS OF HOPE............................19

FLOW ONE 26
FLOW TWO 30
FLOW THREE..34
FLOW FOUR..38
FLOW FIVE 42
FLOW SIX..46

FLOW SEVEN..50
FLOW EIGHT..54
FLOW NINE..58
FLOW TEN..62
FLOW ELEVEN 66
FLOW TWELVE..68

POETIC EXTENSION INTRO................................75
HERE I AM 78
MORE IN THIS SERIES..81
INVITATION TO EXPLORE FURTHER.............84

"There are four houses of hope -
They all look the same"

MESSAGE FROM THE AUTHOR

HOW DOES IT FEEL TO BE HUMAN?

Welcome to this poetic series, which offers an alternative way to examine a philosophy of hope - a philosophy I refer to as the Souls of One's Feet.

This journey began long before I could grasp the depth of its significance. Now, after much turbulence and many transitions, I bring my philosophy to life. Like all human explorations this is going to be turbulent maybe a little uncomfortable.

Souls of One's Feet is about what carries us when nothing else does - a lifelong invitation to hold hope; a vibration that has been at the heart of my musings for over two decades. For me an exploration on what it means to be human.

After much deliberation, observation and exploration, I have concluded that for me, being human is a journey of hope. Over time, I have mused in meanders mapping a poetic series that serve as a bridge to my philosophy. This bridge begins with The Timekeeper... although you may read any of my works in an order you choose...In remembrance that we all arrive in our own space - in time.

Throughout our human journey, we navigate endless avenues of emotion. We seek a middle ground - a harmonious balance - we never quite land in this space, not until we leave this earthly place.

What exactly are we searching for?

Why are we here?

What does it mean to be human?

There exists an empty space I refer to as the 'middle-way' . This is the space, where we pause. The space we feel between our humans experience. These pauses form, what I describe as sequences; sequences I map through my time.

In my observations, hope expands mostly in the sequences of joy. Rarely is it remarked upon in the quieter, more subtle sequences of discomfort. As human beings we dance through light and dark. Through the ebb and flow we call life, we are the dance of existence in time.

Each human experiences time that challenges them, a happening that changes the structure of reality. A loss, a trauma, a profound shift in how it feels to be human. These moments create ripples in frequencies that move through us. If they feel uncomfortable we may avoid-dance. We are always - dancing.

The purpose of these poetic explorations is to illuminate the sequences of hope and formulate a bridge to my life's work a philosophy that comes from my heart. To experience my musings in the hope that is intended I invite you to feel time and space in a way that may appear unusual, uncomfortable, or even uncertain. In this discomfort time expands. Uncertainty deepens our awareness of time, in these spaces we may examine layers of our existence through a lens of hope.

hope

INSPIRATION SURROUNDS US

The heart is not a single room — it is a house of many chambers. Some are filled with light, others with silence. Some echo with laughter long gone, while others wait quietly, untouched, holding the breath of what is yet to come. Within us live whole cities of memory and longing places we return to in dreams, spaces we haven't dared enter. Inspiration surrounds us, inspiration is within us — hidden in the architecture of our soul.

Each chamber of the heart carries its own truth. There is the room of beginnings, where hope flickers. The room of loss, where echoes settle. The room of forgiveness, whose door opens only from within. And above all, the room that is still being built — where you place each moment, each feeling, like a stone upon a stone. We are the builders, the navigators, the ones who light the lanterns and walk barefoot through our own sacred halls. We are the timekeepers in the spaces where hope calls.

This book is a exploration through those inner spaces — a quiet unveiling of what it means to be human and here. These poems are windows, reflections and prayers. They ask nothing of you but time and space. As you wander these pages, may you rediscover the hope that never left — the kind that doesn't shout, but echos gently from within, reminding you that you've always been home. In this space your heart is your sanctuary.

Read along with me on my poetry channel.
Let's journey together through the verses, allowing the words to resonate and unfold.

www.soulsofonesfeet.bandcamp.com

THE UNSEEN CHAMBERS OF HOPE

SOULS OF ONES FEET
A PHILOSOPHY OF HOPE

In the quiet chambers of our hearts, there lies a space where hope resides—an unseen presence, felt deeply within. Hope is an elusive energy, flowing between moments, shimmering in the silence of our most tender thoughts. Houses of Hope invites you to step inside these chambers to witness how hope, like a gentle river, winds its way through our lives, nourishing every corner with grace and love. Even when we cannot feel its vibration - it is gently present ticking in the quiet hours soothing the chambers we hold most dear.

Hope is not always visible, nor loud. It does not demand attention, it moves in the stillness, in the pauses between breaths, in the silent exchange of love that transcends words. It is felt in the touch of a hand, the gaze of another, and in the quiet understanding shared between kindred spirits. Hope is the unseen space - the place where love lingers, where we hold our hearts together - even when the world feels fractured, especially when the world feels fractured.

This poetic journey unfolds across twelve unique philosophical flows, each an exploration on the intricate ways time, nature, and hope intertwine, a perception which is mine, that is my works I bring to life. It is my hope you will come to understand that hope as an energetic vibration is not something we grasp or seek, but something that seeks us - an invisible element that arrives through the channel that is you - and me.

As you move through the chambers of your chest, consider how hope manifests. How does it move you forward, even when you cannot see the path. Through love, through grace, through the simple act of being, hope is always present, always guiding. It is the song of the unseen world, vibrating through the fibres of existence, calling us to listen, to feel, and to honour its quiet strength - our quiet strength.

Hope, like time, is a dance - sometimes slow, sometimes hurried, but always moving. It resides in nature, in the sway of trees, the rhythm of waves, and the changing of seasons. It is the quiet witness to our human journey, the steady hand that holds us through the storms and comforts in the calm. It is not a destination, but a way of being - a feeling. - found between avenues of breathing.

Houses of Hope is a poetic exploration on the unseen energies that shape our lives, a journey through time and nature, and an invitation to recognise that hope is not something to be chased, but something to be felt in the very core of our being. The chambers of your heart through feeling..

What secrets do the chambers of our hearts hold,
if we pause long enough to hear - what do we feel?

FLOW ONE

There are four houses of hope
None of them run linear
The house of Love
 The house of Fear
The house of Joy
 The house of—I am here

Occasionally these meet
In a central space through time
A crossroads—or an avenue
A neighbour passing by
A human interaction—amid times distraction
A middleway—a purpose- an intense reaction
An avenue—a lane
—The light
 The dark
Ambiguous disdain

There are four houses of hope
Yet they all look the same

Objects—entanglements
Bellows and sacraments

We place time into lightwaves
To arrive in peace through hope
The house of love does echoes—as fear does elope
Joy gently arranges
The fragment and the stages—gracefully
Inviting—a guest maybe two
To realign the avenues
We constantly- pursue

There are four houses of hope
Many fragments through space
Yet not one of them—

 None of them—

Hold the space you grace

FLOW TWO

There are four houses of hope
We visit each in passing
Through the times trepid stages
Humanity in phases
A flux—a timeless bellow
The doors they open and lock

Curiosity does echo…

If we knock on the door of fear
An unexpected space we hear
The crowding —the catastrophe
We may run back to the house of I am here
This is our safe space
Our hut or our haven
I am here
 I am here
Time is fear craving
That joy or hope won't venture
There door will remain locked
There are four houses of hope
Where energy does flock

Absorbed and extracted
Computerised
Refracted
Energy—energy
Deliverance is fractured

When we enter the house of fear
Without acceptance of the house of—I am here
We unconsciously flow
Through times trepid glow

Energy—depleted and drained
We furrow—we bellow
We bark and we blame
Projecting with reasoning
Forgetting these houses are all the same

There are four houses of hope
Four chambers in one's heart
That radiate from a central space
No division—no depart

When we sit in stillness
See beyond time and space
We enter the house of humanity
We hold grace
 We hold grace
 We hold grace

FLOW THREE

The are many arenas in time
We flow
 we grow—we wend
The houses of hope gift adventure
To unravel where time might end
Fear is often overcrowded
Riddled with uncertainty and doubt
Blindfolded—crippled
A silenced echoe— shrivelled
A magnetised emotion
A cluttered erosion
A variant in many forms
Projections
Elections
Minor corrections
Reminders
      Disguises
These houses come in many sizes
The walls may swell
A trepid inner yell
The bellow
    The echo
Time will tell
   Time will tell

There are four houses of Hope
They all look the same
Until we illuminate
 Until we investigate
Where the walls begin to crumble
The house of fear falls down
When one holds a heart that's humble

When we enter the house of fear
Without acceptance of the house of—I am here
We unconsciously flow
Through times trepid glow
Energy—depleted and drained

FLOW FOUR

There are four houses of hope
They reside within your heart
You navigate—to Gradiate
This dance of fate—this walk

Heavenly almost human
The house of hope does show

That when love echoes

When time bellows

When hope radiates within

All the houses illuminate
They spiral and they spin...

Time dances

        Time dances

Can you feel your flow sing?

There are four houses of hope
They all feel the same
For the central location
In this elixic rotation
Is not anchored in money nor fame
Temporary measures—of modern human treasures
Buried in times trepid game

Conditions and contracts
Collaborations set the trend
Of how our time should flow

Which way one should wend
Born into confinement
Restrictions and alignment
The doors are locked

The doors are locked
We have a new assignment

There are four houses of hope
They all intertwine
The doors are never locked
Where natures does align

FLOW FIVE

There is an eloquent space
In avenues of grace
Where laughter bounds in brightfulness
 Fear it does fade

Joy—patience and peace

An elevation
       A release

An unexpected avenue
A moment here then gone
As joy does only venture in the moment we belong

Presence
         Passion

An extraction of all fear
As we eloquently tip tiptoe
Through the house of I am here
Joy—
    Gentle joy

There are four houses of hope
Yet I may have to recount
As I step within a middleway
Embark the realms of doubt

Let me out—Let me out

There are many houses of hope
They all feel the same
Anchored on a breath of love
As one unravels the door of shame

I ponder if these are these houses
Or landfills
That once were—
Our narratives
Our additives—
We built in time trepid game

Here I am —here I am-
Reset
    Align
 Reclaim

FLOW SIX

There are many houses of hope
They flow through our human heart

Beating
    Healing
Acknowledging thee depart
We listen—we humanly evolve
To the resonance—the eloquence
The space—as it dissolves
We awaken—through the houses that we hold
Avenues and corridors
Where love and fear fold

We awaken—we open the windows and doors
To examine
    The small print
Of our earthly human flaws

A reality

An emergence

A diluted interference

Hope has put the kettle on
Hope invites us in
When we sit within our stillness —and hold patience within
We evolve—we eloquently evolve
Without there is turbulence
A modern melodic trend
Anxiety —Anxiety
A jargonous path to wend

Labels and fables
Meanders in motion
When we enter the house of hope
All is calm
All is stable

I am back to a beginning
As the sequences they seep
Through time in all its glory
And - the power humans seek

FLOW SEVEN

Time has cleaned the windows
The vision is now clear
When we enter the house of hope
We enter the house of I am here

Love bellows
Patience heals
Joy evolves—
—Time it seals

The frequencies in vibration
The innocuous deliberation
When we awaken—reality does emerge
The house of fear fades
We embark as a creator
Space in all its shades
Purples, pinks in eloquence
The decorator has arrived
To acknowledge in its vibrancy
The walls that have survived

The house of hope illuminates
Joy opens the doors
To remind us with intention
To embrace our human flaws

FLOW EIGHT

There are many houses of hope
There is much to being human
When unravelled from a heart space
To discharge the disillusion
Time is now
Or is time really—nearly now
A cross in exception
Removing the religious interjection
A middleway—a pause
A holding space
A surrender
A groove, that tics and tocs—so slender

ONE
      TWO
            THREE
   FOUR

I am anchored in the centre
We are on the move once more
The light waves
The light waves
The light waves—through the door

There are many houses of hope
Some are undiscovered
Hidden in the avenues ventured by the troubled
The modern world is crumbling
Time anchored—yet rotating
As our ancestors once suggested
Energy is collating

FLOW NINE

There is community
There is compassion
There is spark unearthed in a modern fashion
Objects, erosion
Hope does not flow this way
When we segregate the chambers
We divide— where time does play
Energy in sheathing
Vibrations— underground
As we root within the spirit
Of the houses most profound
I am here
 I am here
In the house held most dear
Through the chambers
The corridors
The avenues of time
I am here
In your heart space
Hopeful and divine

A guest upon arrival
To sit
 To stand—be idle—
Do nothing
Be still
Explore the many houses
Don't rush—or haste
Your time—is your fate

Time has cleaned the windows
The vision is now clear
When we enter the house of hope
We enter the house of I am here

FLOW TEN

There are rows
There are streets
There are crescents which we seek
Yet none of them grace the words which you speak

The landing
    The vibration
Chosen connection gifts of realisation

Hope resides in every home
Every heart and corridor
When we gift it only patience
To breathe— this earthy chore
If we bring awareness to the rhythm of our heart
Where the houses of hope flow
In a effortless kickstart
There is surrender
 There is discomfort
A recoil in calibration
A mesmerising hesitation
A release
A breath in its birth

Yet, amid—the alleyways
The corridors
These avenues in time
 We timelessly purpose
To feel a house that mine

Where are you
How did you arrive?
For the house that you are holding
Is the house that gives you life

FLOW ELEVEN

There are many houses of hope
Mine may not be yours
I hope we've found connected time
Through the space and corridors
In acceptance
In acknowledgement
In removal of judgement and fear
Let us stand united in the house of—I am here
With gratitude and grace
Patience and peace
Let us hold a moment in stillness

Breathe
Now—Release

In awareness that the pathways
We choose to love and wend
May capture time in stillness
Where your heart becomes your friend
A companion in compassion
An embrace in halls that harbour
The mischief and the mayhem
In the house of our father

Remove the jargon
The fearful, doubting, margins
Mother nature she will guide you
Allow your heart to illuminate
As you celebrate the house of hope
As time sways by the gate
The garden it is flourishing
The colours blossom and bloom
For when we enter the house of I am here
We illuminate the room

FLOW TWELVE

There are many houses of hope
Four chambers in your heart
We align through the middleway
To embrace love—as an art

A delicacy—
A vibrant illuminous philosophy
One that is felt—beyond the walls of doubt
Where nothing lands timelessly
In effortless—bellows—felt

Surrender—Surrender
To the chambers of your heart
Where the walls are made with love
In Hope—a graceful start

We are dancing

        We are dancing

Through the purpose of our time
To unravel all the avenues
That connect and intertwine
Wireless connections—
   Electronic defences, misdirections

The maps are too confusing—
 The east and west deluding
That north and south are soothing

For it is thee central location—
 There is no escaping

The purpose of four in your heart—
Delivers right back to the start

You see—
There are four houses of hope
Many fragments through space
Yet non of them—
Not one of them—
Hold the space you grace

There are many houses of hope
Mine may not be yours
I hope we've found connected time
Through the space and corridors

**GRATITUDE & HOPE
LIVE HERE**

HERE I AM

POETIC EXTENSION

It is my heart felt hope that as you have journeyed through this space you felt a pulse between the pages. A pulse that echoes through the chambers of your heart. This rhythm that is you holds an ancient beat, echoes of those who have gone before softly bellowing within all that we are, calling us to remember.

'Here I Am' is not only a reflection on the present moment, but an invitation to acknowledge the time that came before the ancestors who laid the foundations of who we are; within these chambers, these beats of being, are vibrations of hope that expand the passage of time. It is a reminder that the chambers of our hearts are not isolated - each beat reverberates with the wisdom of ages, a timeless flow of consciousness that has always been and will always be within who we are.

HERE I AM

Do not say I do not care
Say I am here—I am there

In order to elevate we separate
The chambers and the contours
The houses and the hope
Through a division known with seven points
A pyramid does evoke
Thought in presentation
Ancestral information
A middleway
 A square
A circle—centred spare
Through the chambers—gentle chambers
—we arrive at—I am there

Here I am
 Here I am
Anchored to time passing
Deliverance
 Deliverance
Earth bound—a bellow in compassion

There are seven points
and many houses of hope
A heptagon is accurately placed
—with its central location at a higher space
A little like ones heart

Chambers —crossroads
—illuminating the dark
Many chambers—Many chambers

Hold space

Breathe

Recalibrate and restart

Here I am—There I am
An accurate contemplation
A human configuration
A memory
 A moment
A meticulous mechanical component
 A septagon
A series
A sequence—they all intertwine
When we meet within a middleway
—in time your there—equals mine
This is the purpose
—of the numerical gifts that surface
Seven points in seven figures
 Four houses held in hope
—and the chambers are sacred chambers
that cast a radiant glow

OTHER WORKS
BY AMY CECILIA GRAINGER

A Philosophy of Hope

The Space Time Lives In
Emerging Through Time and Space

Selected Poetry Collections
The Timekeeper
Houses of Hope
Transforming Trees
Chemistry

CONTINUING THE INQUIRY

HOW DOES IT FEEL TO BE HUMAN?

Thank you for spending time within these poems.

Houses of Hope forms part of a wider body of work exploring time, hope, and human existence through both poetry and philosophy. While these poems approach experience through image and rhythm, the philosophical works examine the same questions through sustained inquiry.

If the reflections within this collection resonate with you, the exploration continues in:

>The Space Time Lives In
>Book I of A Philosophy of Hope

With Love
Amy S

www.ingramcontent.com/pod-product-compliance
Lightning Source LLC
Chambersburg PA
CBHW030455010526
44118CB00011B/945